Antalya Travel Highlights

Best Attractions & Experiences

Deanna Farmer

This publication may not be reproduced, stored in a retrieval system, or transmitted, in any form or by any means without the prior written permission of the publisher. It may not be otherwise circulated in any form of binding or cover other than that in which it is published and without similar condition being imposed on the subsequent purchaser. If there are inaccuracies in copyright acknowledgements the publisher will be pleased to insert the appropriate acknowledgement in subsequent printings of this publication. Although we have taken all reasonable care in researching this book we make no warranty about the accuracy or completeness of its content and disclaim all liability arising from its use.

Copyright © 2022, Astute Press
All Rights Reserved.

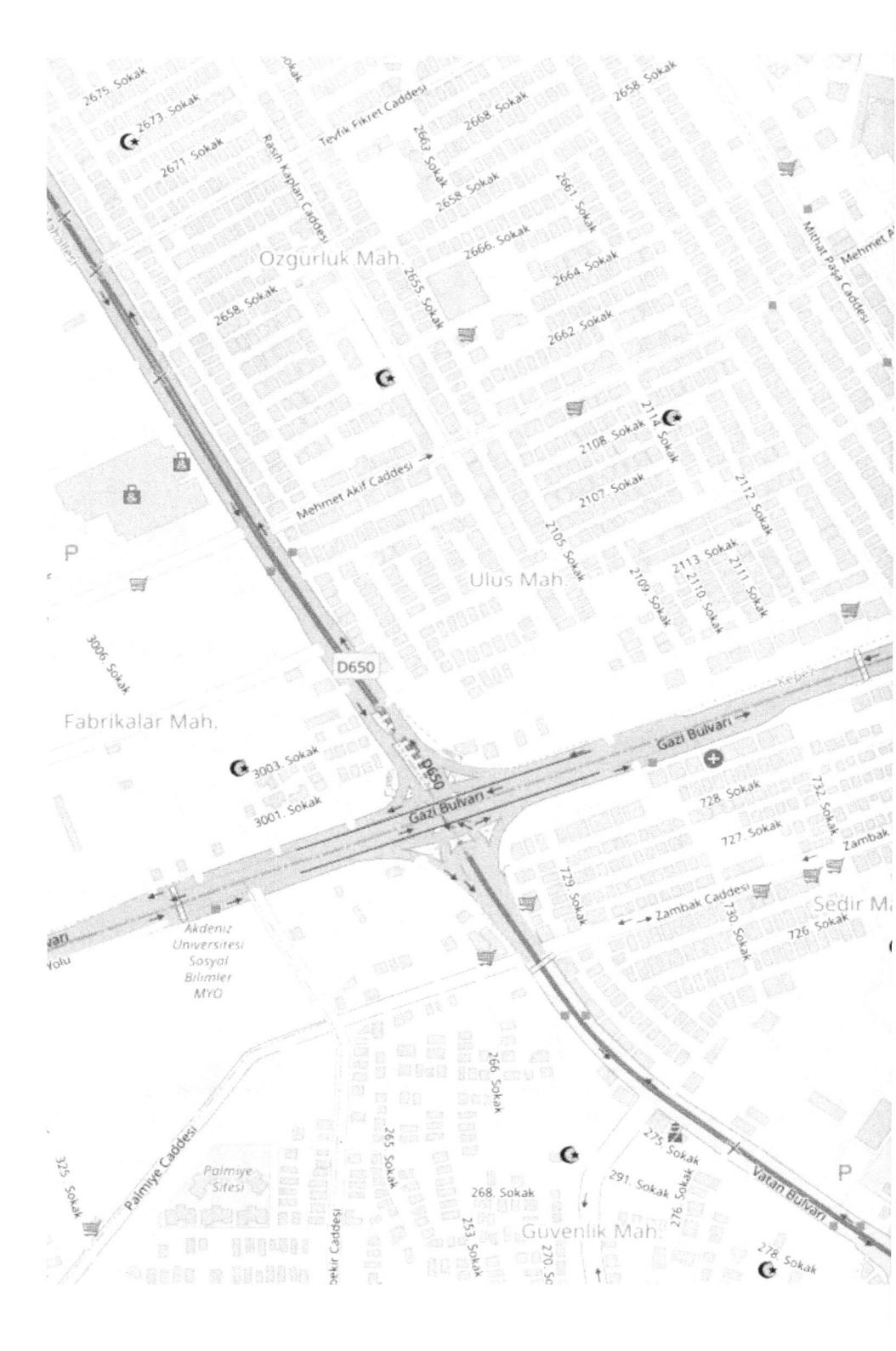

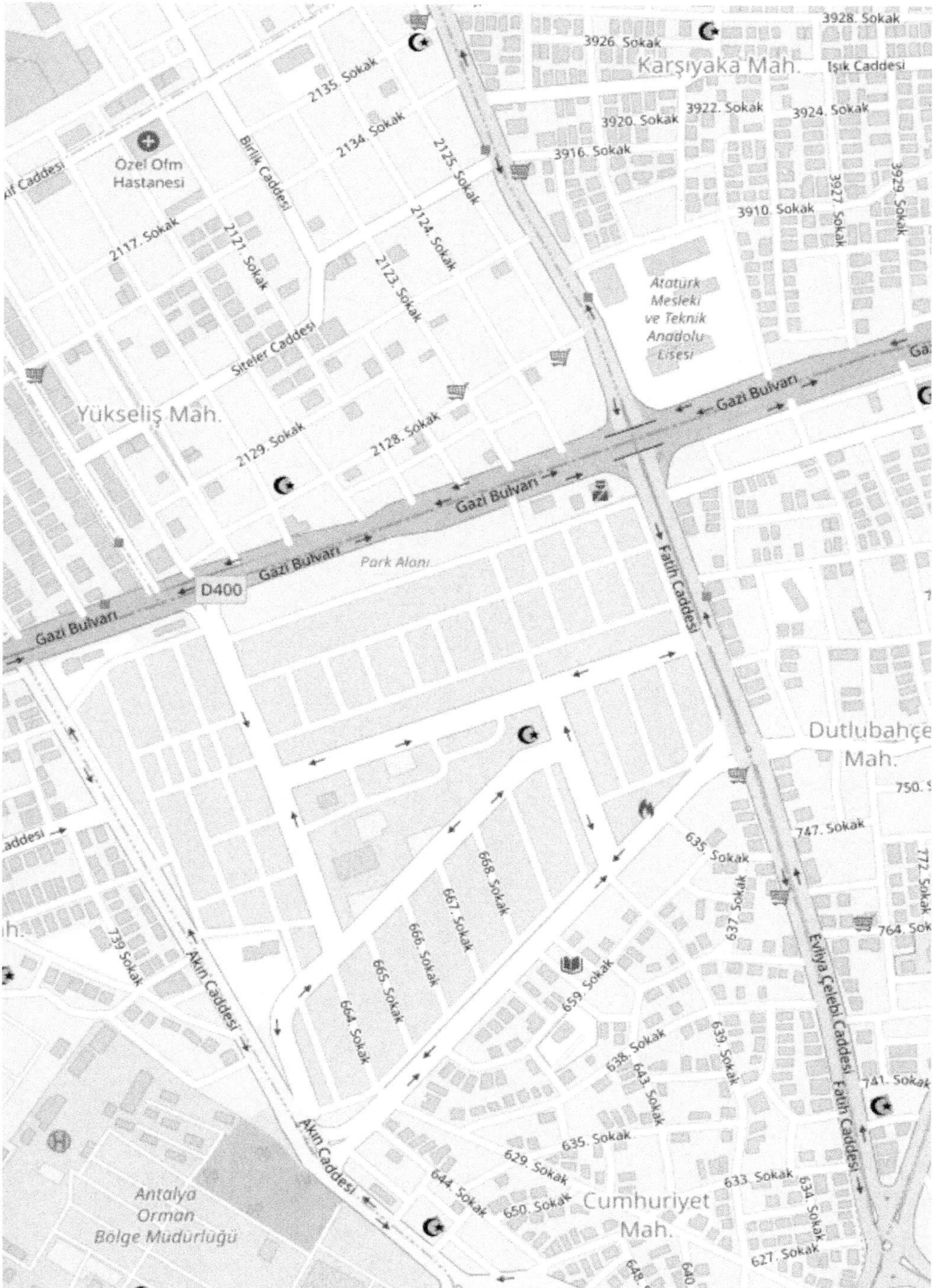

3928. Sokak
3926. Sokak
Karşıyaka Mah.
Işık Caddesi
2135. Sokak
3922. Sokak
3924. Sokak
3920. Sokak
2134. Sokak
Birlik Caddesi
Özel Ofm Hastanesi
2125. Sokak
3916. Sokak
3927. Sokak
3929. Sokak
3910. Sokak
2117. Sokak
2121. Sokak
2124. Sokak
2123. Sokak
Atatürk Mesleki ve Teknik Anadolu Lisesi
Siteler Caddesi
Gazi Bulvarı
Yükseliş Mah.
2129. Sokak
2128. Sokak
Gazi Bulvarı
Park Alanı
Gazi Bulvarı
D400
Fatih Caddesi
Gazi Bulvarı
Dutlubahçe Mah.
747. Sokak
635. Sokak
772. Sokak
668. Sokak
667. Sokak
637. Sokak
764. Sokak
666. Sokak
739. Sokak
Akın Caddesi
665. Sokak
664. Sokak
659. Sokak
639. Sokak
638. Sokak
643. Sokak
Evliya Çelebi Caddesi
741. Sokak
Fatih Caddesi
Akın Caddesi
635. Sokak
629. Sokak
633. Sokak
644. Sokak
634. Sokak
Antalya Orman Bölge Müdürlüğü
650. Sokak
Cumhuriyet Mah.
627. Sokak
648. Sokak
640. Sokak

Contents

	Page
Welcome to Antalya	7
☐ 1. Perge Archaeological Site	7
☐ 2. Hadrian's Gate	8
☐ 3. Aspendos Theater	9
☐ 4. Kaleiçi Old Town	10
☐ 5. Karain Cave	11
☐ 6. Konyaalti Beach	12
☐ 7. Düden Waterfall	12
☐ 8. Hıdırlık Tower	14
☐ 9. Manavgat Waterfall	15
☐ 10. Antalya Clock Tower	15
☐ 11. Göynük Canyon	17
☐ 12. Karaalioglu Park	17
☐ 13. Antalya Old Port	19
☐ 14. Antalya Aquarium	19
☐ 15. Temple of Apollo	20
☐ 16. Antalya Tünektepe Teleferik	21
☐ 17. Selge Ruins	21
☐ 18. Mark Antalya Shopping Mall	22
☐ 19. MiniCity Antalya	23
☐ 20. Broken Minaret Mosque	24
☐ 21. Antalya Archeological Museum	25

- 22. Perge Theatre 26
- 23. Atatürk Park 26
- 24. Antalya Zoo 27
- 25. Old Bazaar 28
- 26. Seleucia 29
- 27. Eurymedon Bridge 30
- 28. Aktur Lunapark 30
- 29. Lycian Way 31
- 30. Cumhuriyet Meydanı Park 31
- 31. Kundu Bazaar 32

Picture Credits 32

Welcome to Antalya

Located on the southern coast of Turkey, Antalya is a stunning port city rich in history and steeped in culture. Famous for its massive Roman amphitheater, Kaleiçi historic district, and pristine beaches, this resort city is a popular vacation spot. With countless restaurants and shopping venues to choose from, there's no shortage of things to do.

☐ 1. Perge Archaeological Site

Address: Aksu 07110, Turkey
Phone: +90 242 247 76 60
Email: antalya@kulturturizm.gov.tr
Wikipedia: https://en.wikipedia.org/wiki/Perga

The ruins of Perga include ancient structures from the Hellenistic, Roman and Byzantine periods. The most impressive among them is a theatre, seating 2300 people in 43 rows; it dates back to the 2nd century BCE. There are also remains of the agoras, basilicas, thermae and temples. Somewhat apart from the town there is a rock with an inscription recording the privileges which were granted by the Roman emperors to ancient Perateia.

☐ 2. Hadrian's Gate

Address: Barbaros Mh., Kaleiçi, 07100 Antalya, Turkey

Hadrian's Gate (otherwise known as the Middle Gate) is a triumphal arch in Antalya built in honor of the Roman Emperor Hadrian. It was constructed between AD 130 and 131 on an outcrop to a height of over 12 meters. Its total span is 15 meters;

it has three openings across, and two side passages at a height of 3.5 m from the ground The gate still stands today with one post missing due to damage caused by an earthquake in 1508.

☐ 3. Aspendos Theater

Phone: +90 242 247 76 60
Email: antalya@kulturturizm.gov.tr

The Aspendos theater in Antalya is a symbol of Roman architectural splendor. The theatre was built in the ancient city of Aspendos in 189 BC by a Greek architect Zeno of Pergamon during the rule of Eumenes II.

☐ 4. Kaleiçi Old Town

Address: 62 Uzunçarşı Sokak, Muratpaşa 07100, Turkey

Kaleiçi is the historic district of Antalya. Until modern times, almost all of the city was confined within its walls. Today it has structures dating from Roman, Byzantine, Seljuk, Ottoman and modern Turkish republican eras. Kaleiçi's narrow walkways are atmospheric and filled with history. This time inspired by the past and overlooking the Mediterranean Sea, Kaleiçi remains one of the most popular areas for any visitor to relax and enjoy delicious mezes in one of the local restaurants.

☐ 5. Karain Cave

On the Dilek Peninsula, in Yumurtalık district of Antalya province there are several paleolithic sites. According to radiocarbon dating, the oldest ones are more than 50,000 years old. Among them, the site called "Cave of the Paleolithic Art" is a cave that contains detailed and strikingly colored wall paintings. In the cave are depicted human figures, hunting scenes and animal drawings on every surface of the walls and ceiling. The animal depicted are so-called "ice age animals" such as lions, elephants and rhinoceroses.

☐ 6. Konyaalti Beach

Konyaalti Beach is the most popular and one of the world's most beautiful beaches. Located right in the heart of Antalya, it is very convenient to get to and perfect for both locals and tourists. It offers all modern facilities with free parking and Wi-Fi connections. Konyaalti Beach which is lined with restaurants, cafes, pubs, discos, clubs and shops is a lively place throughout the year.

☐ 7. Düden Waterfall

Address: Lara Caddesi, Muratpaşa 07230, Turkey

Düden Waterfalls are a picturesque series of waterfalls near the city of Antalya. The area can be viewed from the impressive Lara Beach. The powerful waterfalls have carved a well-sized canyon, which is also worth seeing. The nearby River Düden flows into the Mediterranean Sea.

☐ 8. Hıdırlık Tower

Address: Kılınçarslan, 07100 Antalya, Turkey

Hıdırlık Tower was built in the 2nd century CE. It is situated at the southern side of Antalya, where the land walls of Hadrian's Gate meet the sea walls. It was constructed by the Roman Empire and later turned into a circular tower. It was named after a Turkish knight, "Hıdicilik", who fought in the city.

☐ 9. Manavgat Waterfall

Manavgat Waterfall is one of the most beautiful natural attractions in Turkey. The waterfall is located 3 km from Manavgat, near Side, on the Manavgat River. It is best viewed from a high altitude and its white, foaming water flows powerfully over the rocks. There are shady tea gardens near the waterfalls providing a pleasant resting place.

The waterfall featured on the old Turkish banknotes during the 1970s.

☐ 10. Antalya Clock Tower

Address: 34 Cumhuriyet Caddesi, Muratpaşa 07040, Turkey

The Antalya Clock Tower is an ancient landmark in Antalya. This tower was a part of the city walls that surrounded the town during the Byzantine Empire. The 120 meter-high structure was built in the early 18th century in honor of Ottoman Sultan Abdul Hamid I, and it has undergone several renovations throughout the years.

☐ 11. Göynük Canyon

The Göynük Canyon is a gorge in Turkey's Mediterranean region known as the "deepest canyon" in the world. The canyon is located inside the Beydağları Coastal National Park, about 4km to Göynük Village of Kemer District in Antalya Province. The 4.5km-long canyon is an important part of the long-distance trail Lycian Way. There is a waterfall and ponds inside the gorge and it offers outdoor recreational activities such as hiking and bird watching.

☐ 12. Karaalioglu Park

Address: Muratpaşa 07100, Turkey

Karaalioğlu Park is a large park in Antalya. It is just south of Kaleiçi in the city center, easily reached on foot or by tram. The mayor's office, Municipal city theater, and an ancient fort called Hıdırlık Tower overlooking the Roman harbor, view of the cliffs and the broad blue expanse of the Gulf of Antalya are major attractions of the park.

☐ 13. Antalya Old Port

Antalya Old City is a place of history that is waiting to be explored. In the shadow of the Old Port, a major port in Roman times, the old city is the heart of today's Antalya. Today, with its museums, restaurants and shops, it still has an air of mystery in which you can enjoy an authentic Turkish coffee or a tasty dish made from the seafood that comes fresh from the Mediterranean Sea.

☐ 14. Antalya Aquarium

Address: Dumlupınar Bulvarı Arapsuyu Mahallesi 502, Konyaaltı, 07200 Antalya, Turkey
Phone: +90 242 245 6565
Email: info@antalyaaquarium.com

Web: http://www.antalyaaquarium.com/

Antalya Aquarium showcases marine and freshwater life in Europe's largest cylinder-shaped aquarium, as well as other tanks built in the ark-style. The site also features the world's first tunnel aquarium which takes visitors on a trip through history, and a snow world that includes penguin and polar bear shows.

☐ 15. Temple of Apollo

Address: Barbaros Cd, 07600 Side/Antalya Province, Turkey

The Temple of Apollo lies just eight kilometers from Turkey's Mediterranean city Antalya. It is worth visiting the site in daytime as well as at sunset. From its location at the center of the Mediterranean, a stream of light falls right on the temple's podium. As a whole, the ruins make a magical sight when seen against the sapphire-blue skies and golden sunsets that ensue after a day on Turkey's unspoiled, sandy beaches.

☐ 16. Antalya Tünektepe Teleferik

The Antalya Tünektepe Teleferik is the original funicular railway that goes up Tünektepe Hill that is located to the west of Antalya.

☐ 17. Selge Ruins

Wikipedia: https://en.wikipedia.org/wiki/Selge

The ruins of Selge date back to the third millennium BCE. It underwent changes of importance in the periods of Arzawa, Hittites, Achaemenid, Ancient Greek, Roman, Byzantine and Turkish rulers and was finally abandoned in the 19th century. The city extended over two plateaux at an elevation of 400 m (1,312 ft) above sea level, covering an area of approximately 100 hectares (247 acres).

☐ 18. Mark Antalya Shopping Mall

Address: Tahılpazarı Mah. Kazım Özalp Caddesi (Şarampol) No:88, 07100 Antalya, Turkey
Phone: +90 242 244 6666
Email: info@markantalya.com
Web: https://twitter.com/MarkAntalyaavm

Web: http://www.markantalya.com/en/index.html

The Mark Antalya is a large shopping mall offering numerous boutiques and a cinema. Try on the latest fashions in their chic boutiques before dining in one of their restaurants The Mark Antalya mall is located at the heart of the old town center in Kaleici, Antalya.

☐ 19. MiniCity Antalya

Address: Meltem Mh., 601. Sk, 07030 Antalya/Antalya Province, Turkey
Phone: +90 242 229 45 45
Web: http://minicitypark.com/

MiniCity Antalya is a miniature city playground that is perfect for toddlers and up. With an area of 1 square kilometer, you'll likely get lost looking for Sümela monastery in the Armenian mountains or some of the iconic buildings of Istanbul.

☐ 20. Broken Minaret Mosque

Address: 14 424. Sokak, Muratpaşa 07040, Turkey

The Kesik Minare Cami (Broken Minaret Mosque) is located in the Kaleiçi (old town) of Antalya's Konyaaltı quarter. It was built as a Roman temple in the 2nd century AD and then converted into a Byzantine church in the 7th century. The building was damaged during the Arab invasions in the 7th century and then repaired in the 9th century. It was turned into a mosque by Caliph Mahmut ibn Tulun, but it was abandoned after an earthquake in 1857.

☐ 21. Antalya Archeological Museum

Address: Konyaaltı Cad 1, 07050 Antalya, Turkey
Phone: +90 242 238 5688
Email: info@antalyamuzesi.gov.tr
Web: http://www.antalyamuzesi.gov.tr/

The Antalya Archaeological Museum, with its 13 exhibition halls and large open air gallery, introduces visitors to the history of Turkey and the Mediterranean region. It includes a display of some 5,000 finds from regions as far apart as Afghanistan and Spain. The museum's origins go back to 1888 when the Ottoman authorities displayed findings from archaeological excavations in the city of Antalya in an exhibition in Konyaaltı. In 1966, work started on the building that houses the current museum, which was opened in 1970.

22. Perge Theatre

Address: Perge Caddesi, Aksu 07110, Turkey

The Perge Theatre is a multi-purpose venue in Antalya. Completed in 2009, it was designed by Merih Mutlu, an architect from Perge ancient city in Antalya and uses the marble columns and reliefs discovered during regional excavations. The theatre holds 1,100 visitors.

23. Atatürk Park

Address: Muratpaşa 07050, Turkey

Atatürk Park is a public park in Mersin, Turkey honoring the memory of Mustafa Kemal Atatürk, the founder and first President of the Republic of Turkey. Inaugurated on 29 May 1977, the park covers an area of 25 acres (10 ha) in Gülnar district near the Mersin Marina. It features historical monuments in addition to 110 different species of trees and plants.

☐ 24. Antalya Zoo

Address: Kepez Piknik Sahası İçerisi, Kepez, Antalya, Turkey
Phone: 0242 322 3232
Email: antalyazoo@antalya.bel.tr
Web: http://antalya.bel.tr/antalyazoo/

The Antalya Zoo is a must-see for the whole family. It features many wild animals, including ibexes and deer, as well as ostriches and zebras. The zoo has various monkeys and hosts a petting area to give visitors a chance to get up close to rabbits, kangaroos and goats. When you're finished enjoying the animals, head to the outdoor cafés located within the grounds.

☐ 25. Old Bazaar

Address: 6 İsmetpaşa Caddesi, Muratpaşa 07040, Turkey

The Old Bazaar in Antalya is one of the city's historical landmarks and a notable tourist attraction. The main parts of the bazaar are its 2 large streets, İskele Avenue (the wharf road) and İncili Çarşı Caddesi (the Incil Street), which are lined with unique shops.

The bazaar covers a maze of narrow alleys and streets, lined with picturesque architecture.

☐ 26. Seleucia

Seleucia was a harbor city on the Mediterranean coast of Asia Minor. It was the main port of the Pamphylian region. This 2200 year old city today includes impressive cliffs, ruins and archeological sites spread along a 3 kilometer coastline with ancient tombs, temples, baths, a stadium and agora. The most interesting sight is the majestic theater that sits atop Mt Dikeos.

☐ 27. Eurymedon Bridge

The Eurymedon Bridge, Antalya was built during the Roman Empire in the 2nd century AD. Part of a former international trading route to Persia leading through Selge, this segment spans over 300 m and features 9 semi-circular arches built of limestone blocks.

☐ 28. Aktur Lunapark

Address: Konyaaltı 07070, Turkey
Phone: +90 242 229 1984
Email: info@akturpark.com
Web: http://www.akturpark.com.tr/

Lunapark Antalya is one of the best amusement parks in Turkey. Having an area of 2 hectares, the theme park has roller coasters, spinning rides, merry-go-rounds and water slides. Its magnificent Ferris wheel provides breathtaking views of the city and surrounding areas.

☐ 29. Lycian Way

The Lycian Way is a long-distance hiking trail in Turkey around part of the coast of ancient Lycia. Over 500 km long, it goes from Ölüdeniz, near Fethiye, to Geyikbayırı, about 20 kilometers from Antalya.

The trail's placemarkers are painted with red and white stripes. The trail is an ancient cobbled pathway that winds through mountains and valleys and provides access to scattered ruins along the way.

Some of these sites date back almost 3,000 years and give you a glimpse into the island's history.

☐ 30. Cumhuriyet Meydanı Park

Address: 78 21. Sokak, Muratpaşa 07100, Turkey

Cumhuriyet Meydanı, Antalya is one of Turkey's grand central parks. There are historical monuments, fountains and cafes located in the middle of this meydan, which is surrounded by sandstone buildings.

☐ 31. Kundu Bazaar

Address: Tesisler Caddesi, Kundu 07110, Turkey

Eat, drink and shop your way through one of Antalya's famous shopping centers. Just a few steps away from the beachfront promenade lies Kundu Bazaar. The perfect spot to browse wares ranging from authentic carpets and Turkish rugs to luxurious alpaca garments. Step inside the intricate maze of small shops that wind through the sunken garden courtyards, or unwind with a drink in the quaint kahvehanes (traditional coffeehouses).

Picture Credits

Antalya, Turkey Cover: slh-altuntas / 6487991 (Pixabay)
Perge Archaeological Site: Seynaeve René (CC BY-SA 3.0)
Hadrian's Gate: Bernard Gagnon (CC BY-SA 3.0)
Aspendos Theater: Saffron Blaze (CC BY-SA 3.0)
Kaleiçi Old Town: Cobija (CC0)
Karain Cave: Ingo Mehling (CC BY-SA 3.0)
Düden Waterfall: Saffron Blaze (CC BY 3.0)

Hıdırlık Tower: Bernard Gagnon (CC BY-SA 3.0)
Manavgat Waterfall: Thomas Gensler (CC BY-SA 2.0 de)
Antalya Clock Tower: Quevero (CC BY-SA 3.0)
Göynük Canyon: Brbbl (GFDL)
Karaalioglu Park: Ont (PD)
Antalya Old Port: Henkiedenkie (CC BY-SA 3.0)
Temple of Apollo: Heribert Pohl — Thanks For Half A Million Clicks! (CC BY-SA 2.0)
Selge Ruins: Allie_Caulfield (CC BY 2.0)
Mark Antalya Shopping Mall: Cobija (CC BY-SA 4.0)
Broken Minaret Mosque: Ingo Mehling (CC BY-SA 3.0)
Antalya Archeological Museum: E-92 In Turkish Wikipedia (PD)
Perge Theatre: Rene Nueesch (CC BY 3.0)
Atatürk Park: Sinan Şahin (CC BY 3.0)
Seleucia: Dosseman (CC BY-SA 4.0)
Eurymedon Bridge: Ralf Rochow (CC BY-SA 3.0)
Aktur Lunapark: Ufukonen (CC BY 3.0)
Lycian Way: Myname (Knut Thieme) (CC BY-SA 2.0 de)

Printed in Great Britain
by Amazon